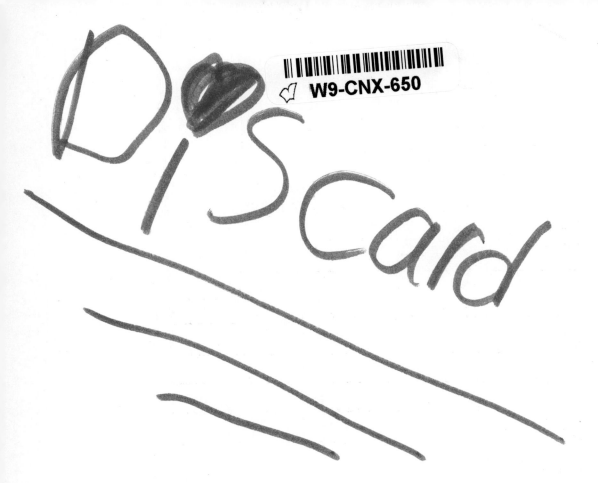

W9-CNX-650

1

Scott Foresman

Accelerating English Language Learning

Authors

Anna Uhl Chamot

Jim Cummins

Carolyn Kessler

J. Michael O'Malley

Lily Wong Fillmore

Consultant

George González

Longman

ACKNOWLEDGMENTS

Illustrations Unless otherwise acknowledged, all illustrations are the property of Scott, Foresman and Company. Page abbreviations are as follows: (T) top, (B) bottom, (L) left, (R) right, (C) center.

Lisa Adams 62, 72–73; Elizabeth Allen 10–11, 18–19, 39, 40–41, 46, 70–71, 77, 80–81, 102–103, 118–119, 142–143, 180, 186–187, 197, 211; Lee Lee Brazeal 38, 64–65, 204; Ruth Bornstein 26–37; John Burgoyne 104, 105, 208–209; Patrice Rossi Calkin 231; Ruta Daugavietis 138, 233; Paul Dolan 114, 202–203; Bob Dorsey 161; Ebet Dudley 146; Lane DuPont 76; 140–141, 148–149, 194–195; James Endicott 216–227; Lane Gregory 193, 234–235, 236; Yumi Heo 88–99; Todd Leonardo 15; Jill Murphy 164–175; Anita Nelson 86–87, 108–109, 176, 184–185, 206–207, 213; Cheryl Roberts 66–69, 100, 122, 156–157, 190; John Sandford 24–25, 42–43, 83, 84, 120–121, 150–152, 200–201, 228; Janice Skivington 6–9, 44–45, 63; Susan Spellman 16–17, 48–49, 110–111, 116–117, 188–189; Three Communication Design 12–13, 74–75, 115, 123; Elaine Wadsworth 4–5; Nadine Bernard Westcott 126–137.

Literature 26-37: LITTLE GORILLA by Ruth Borstein. Copyright © 1976 Seabury Press. Reprinted by permission. 50-61: MY SCHOOL, YOUR SCHOOL by Bette Birnbaum. Copyright © 1990 American Teachers Publications. Reprinted by permission of Raintree/Steck-Vaughn Publishers. 88-99: ONE AFTERNOON by Yumi Heo. Copyright © 1994 by Yumi Heo. All rights reserved. Reprinted by permission of Orchard Books, New York. 126-137: From THE LADY WITH THE ALLIGATOR PURSE by Nadine Bernard Westcott. Copyright © 1988 by Nadine Bernard Westcott. Reprinted by permission of Little, Brown and Company. 164-175: From PEACE AT LAST by Jill Murphy. Copyright © 1980 by Jill Murphy. Reprinted by permission of Dial Books for Young Readers, a division of Penguin Books USA Inc. 216-227: TREES by Harry Behn, illustrated by James Endicott. Copyright 1949 by Harry Behn. Copyright © renewed 1977 by Alice L. Behn. Illustrations copyright © 1992 by James Endicott. A Bill Martin Book for Henry Holt and CO., Inc. Reprinted by permission of Marian Reiner and Henry Holt and Co., Inc.

Poems and Songs 14: "My Baby Brother" from FATHERS, MOTHERS, SISTERS, BROTHERS: A COLLECTION OF FAMILY POEMS by Mary Ann Hoberman. Text copyright © 1991 by Mary Ann Hoberman. Reprinted by permission of Little, Brown and Company. 38: "Everything Grows" by Raffi. 62: From "The First Day of School" by Sarah Wilson. Reprinted by permission of Edythea Ginis Selman Literary Agency Inc. 76: "If You're Happy and You Know It" from SALLY GO ROUND THE SUN by Edith Fowke. Text copyright © 1969 McClelland and Stewart Ltd. Reprinted by permission of McClelland and Stewart Ltd., Canada. 100: "My Street" words and music by Malvina Reynolds from THERE'S MUSIC IN THE AIR by Malvina Reynolds. Copyright © 1972 Schroder Music Co. (ASCAP) All rights reserved. Reprinted by permission of Schroder Music Co. 138: "Look Both Ways" by Dee Lillegard from HUMPTY DUMPTY'S MAGAZINE. Copyright © 1984 by Children's Better Health Institute, Benjamin Franklin Literary & Medical Society, Inc., Indianapolis, Indiana. Reprinted by permission. 150-152: "Allie Alligator" by Babs Bell Hajdusiewicz, illustrated by John Sanford from SCOTT FORESMAN HOLISTIC TESTS, Grade 1. Copyright © 1995 ScottForesman and Company. 176: "The Bear Went Over the Mountain" from TOM TINKER CHIN CHOPPER by Tom Glazer. Copyright © 1973 Songs and Music, Inc. Reprinted by permission. 190: "The Clap and Quiet Poem" from SEPTEMBER TO SEPTEMBER by Dee Lillegard. Copyright © 1986 by Regensteiner Publishing Enterprises, Inc. Published by Childrens Press. Reprinted by permission of Grolier Publishing Co. 204: "You'll Sing a Song" by Ella Jenkins. 228: "Shadows" from JUST AROUND THE CORNER by Leland B. Jacobs, Revised Edition. Text copyright © 1993 by Allan D. Jacobs. Reprinted by permission of Henry Holt and Co., Inc.

Photography Unless otherwise acknowledged, all photographs are the property of Scott, Foresman and Company. Page abbreviations are as follows: (T) top, (C) center, (B) bottom, (R) right.

v(r) Superstock; v(l) Lawrence Migdale; 2(b), 3(b) Superstock, Inc.; 3(t) Lawrence Migdale; 6–7, 8–9 Courtesy Musem of New Mexico, Photo by Wyatt Davis, Neg. 11567; 14 Superstock, Inc.; 21 Tony Porto; 23(b) National Audubon Society/Photo Researchers; (t) Paul Freed/Animals Animals; 47 Myrleen Ferguson/PhotoEdit; 50, 51 Michael Heron; 52, 54, 55, 56, 57 Lawrence Migdale; 53(t, b) Richard Hutchings/PhotoEdit; 58(t, b) Lea/OMNI-Photo Communications, Inc.; 59(t, b) Michael Heron; 60, 61 Ted Horowitz/Stock Market; 78(t, c), 79(t, b), 106(t, b), 107(t) Superstock, Inc.; 109(t, b) Don & Pat Valenti; 109(c), 112, 125(r) Superstock, Inc.; 125(l) David Young-Wolff/PhotoEdit; 154(bl) Gary Benson/Tony Stone Images; (t) Superstock, Inc.; (br) Jonathan Nourok/PhotoEdit; 158(br,tr), 159(tl, tr) Superstock, Inc.; 179(cr) Don & Pat Valenti; (c l, bl, br) Superstock, Inc.; 181(br) Don & Pat Valenti; 181(tr,bl), 182(bl,cr,cl), 183(tr, bl, br, cr) Superstock, Inc.; 212(t) Mark Lewis/Tony Stone Images; (b) Superstock, Inc.; (c) Photri, Inc.

ISBN: 0-13-027486-0

Copyright © 2001, 1997 Scott, Foresman and Company
All Rights Reserved. Printed in the United States of America.

This publication is protected by Copyright and permission should be obtained from the publisher prior to any prohibited reproduction, storage in a retrieval system, or transmission in any form or by any means, electronic, mechanical, photocopying, recording, or otherwise.
For information regarding permission, write to:
Pearson Education
10 Bank Street, White Plains, NY 10606

3 4 5 6 7 8 9 10—KR—05 04 03 02 01

CONSULTANTS

Sandra H. Bible
Elementary ESL Teacher
Shawnee Mission School District
Shawnee Mission, Kansas

Anaida Colón-Muñiz, Ed.D.
Director of English Language
Development
and Bilingual Education
Santa Ana Unified School District
Santa Ana, California

Debbie Corkey-Corber
Educational Consultant
Williamsburg, Virginia

**Barbara Crandall
Carol Baranyi
Ilean Zamlut**
ESOL Teachers
Lake Park Elementary School
Palm Beach County, Florida

Lily Pham Dam
Instructional Specialist
Dallas Independent School District
Dallas, Texas

María Delgado
Milwaukee Public Schools
Milwaukee, Wisconsin

Dr. M. Viramontes de Marín
Chair, Department of Education and
Liberal Studies at the National
Hispanic University
San Jose, California

Virginia Hansen
ESOL Resource Teacher
Palm Beach County, Florida

Tim Hart
Supervisor of English as a Second
Language
Wake County
Releigh, North Carolina

Lilian I. Jezik
Bilingual Resource Teacher
Corona-Norco Unified School District
Norco, California

Helen L. Lin
Chairman, Education Program
Multicultural Arts Council of
Orange County, California
Formerly ESL Lab Director,
Kansas City, Kansas Schools

**Justine McDonough
Trish Lirio
Sheree Di Donato**
Jupiter Elementary School
West Palm Beach, Florida

Teresa Montaña
United Teachers Los Angeles
Los Angeles, California

Loriana M. Novoa, Ed.D.
Research and Evaluation Consultants
Miami, Florida

Beatrice Palls
ESOL and Foreign Language
Supervisor
Pasco County, Florida

Rosa María Peña
Austin Independent School District
Austin, Texas

Alice Quarles
Assistant Principal
Fairlawn Elementary School
Dade County, Florida

Thuy Pham-Remmele
ESL/Bilingual K–12 Specialist
Madison Metropolitan School District
Madison, Wisconsin

Jacqueline J. Servi Margis
ESL and Foreign Language
Curriculum Specialist
Milwaukee Public Schools
Milwaukee, Wisconsin

Carmen Sorondo
Supervisor, ESOL, K–12
Hillsborough County, Florida

Susan C. VanLeuven
Poudre R-1 School District
Fort Collins, Colorado

Rosaura Villaseñor
(Educator)
Norwalk, California

Cheryl Wilkinson
J. O. Davis Elementary School
Irving Independent School District
Irving, Texas

Phyllis I. Ziegler
ESL/Bilingual Consultant
New York, New York

TABLE OF CONTENTS

Tell what you know.

Who is in each **family?**

Families

Talk About It

Draw your family.
Describe your
family.

What do families do?

Word Bank

care

hug

listen

share

Families eat together.

Families help each other.

Families work and play together.

Family members show they love each other.

Talk About It

What does your family do together?

Work of Long Ago

Some families worked on farms.

They grew plants for food.

They raised animals for food.

Mothers made clothes.

Children helped.

Fathers made furniture.

Children helped.

 **Draw About It**

How do you help your family?

Draw a picture to show what you do.

Fun of Long Ago

Families invited friends to visit.

They ate together.

They danced.

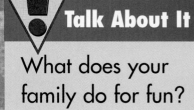

Talk About It

What does your family do for fun?

Peter's family changes.

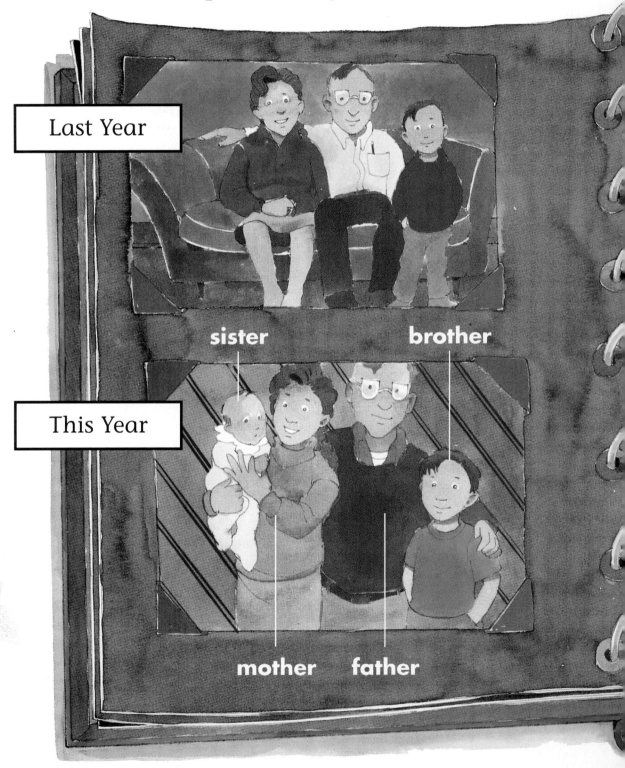

Last Year

This Year

sister

brother

mother   father

Peter's New Sister

Sometimes Peter plays with his sister.

Sometimes Peter plays with friends.

Think About It

How is your family growing and changing?

Tell a friend how you have changed since last year.

My Family

by Juan Castro, age 6

This is my family. This is my father,
my mother, Becky, and Pablo.

I have fun at the pool
with my brother.

My family likes to dance.

My
Baby Brother

by Mary Ann Hoberman

My baby brother's beautiful,
So perfect and so tiny.
His skin is soft and velvet brown;
His eyes are dark and shiny.

His hair is black and curled up tight;
His two new teeth are sharp and white.
I like it when he chews his toes;
And when he laughs, his dimple shows.

Draw About It

Draw a picture of someone in your family.

Tell what you learned.

1. Who is in this family?

2. How are they helping each other?

3. What do you do with your family?
Draw a picture. Tell a friend about
your drawing.

Growing and Changing

Tell what you know.

How do you know you have grown?

▲ I am **bigger.**

◀ I am **taller.**

What new things can they do?

He can ride his ▶
bike now.

She can hit a ball. ▲

Talk About It

What new things
can you do?

How do children grow?

When you were a **baby** you were very **small.**

1 year old

2 years old

3 years old

You grew and grew.

4 years old

5 years old

6 years old

Now you are **bigger** and **taller.**

When you were a baby, you could not do many things.

Now you are bigger. You have changed. You can do many things.

I can tie my shoe.

I can write my name.

I can jump rope.

Mary

I can whistle.

Think About It

Name things babies cannot do.

How big are your hands?

Which hand print is bigger?

Which hand print is smaller?

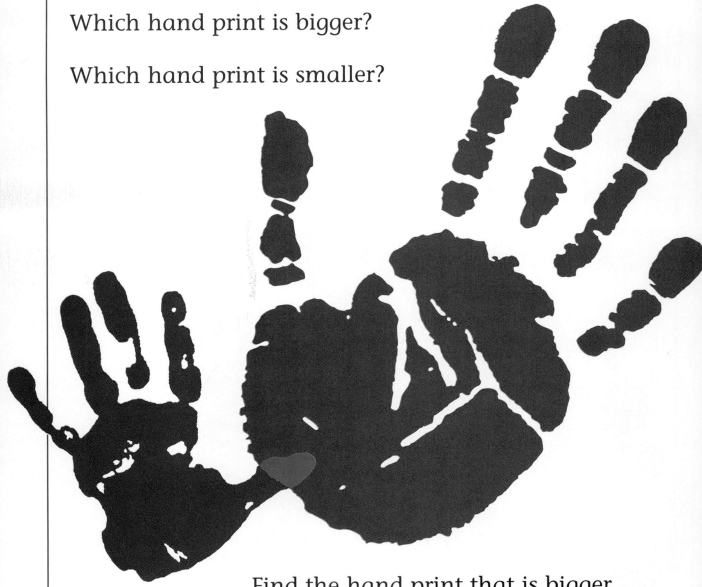

Find the hand print that is bigger than your hand.

Find the hand print that is smaller than your hand.

Have your teeth changed?

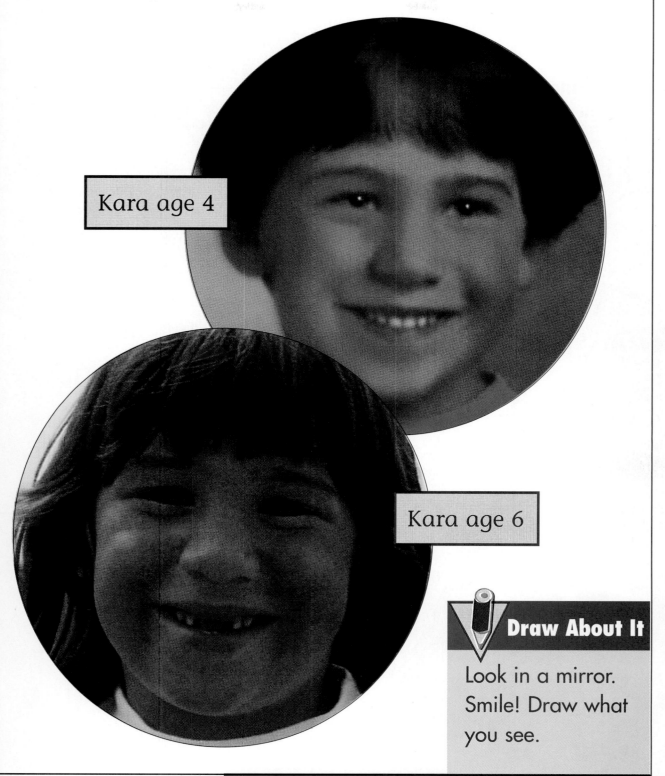

Kara age 4

Kara age 6

Draw About It

Look in a mirror. Smile! Draw what you see.

Make a home for mealworms.

Things You Need

tape

apple slice

oatmeal

mealworms

plastic container with lid

Follow these steps.

1. Put some oatmeal into the container.

2. Place an apple slice into the container.

3. Put mealworms into the container. Tape on the lid.

4. Put the home in a warm place away from sunlight.

Watch mealworms grow and change.

pupa

beetle

Things You Need

 mealworm home

 hand lens

mealworms

 crayons

Follow these steps.

1. Place a mealworm on a paper.

2. Look at the mealworm with the hand lens.

3. Watch the mealworm for 14 days. Watch the color, size, and shape change.

Draw About It

Draw two pictures. Show how the mealworms look the first day. Show how the mealworms look the last day.

Measure animals in the spring.

Word Bank

inch

ruler

How long is the turtle?

How long is the yellow fish?

How long is the pink fish?

Use a string to help you measure.

Measure animals in the fall.

Did the turtle grow longer?

Did the yellow fish grow longer?

Did the pink fish grow longer?

How much did each animal grow?

Think About It

What other animals live in water?

Little Gorilla

Story and Pictures by Ruth Bornstein

Once there was a little gorilla, and everybody loved him. His mother loved him. His father loved him.

His grandma and grandpa, and his aunts and uncles loved him. Even when he was only one day old, everybody loved Little Gorilla.

Pink Butterfly flying through the forest,

Green Parrot in his tree, and Red Monkey in her tree, all loved Little Gorilla.

Even Big Boa Constrictor thought Little Gorilla was nice.

Giraffe, walking tall through the forest, was there when Little Gorilla needed him. Young Elephant, and Old Elephant too, came to see him.

Lion roared his loudest roar for him. Even Old Hippo took him wherever he wanted to go, because she loved Little Gorilla.

Just about everybody in the great green forest
loved Little Gorilla!

Then one day something happened . . . Little
Gorilla began to grow and Grow

and Grow and GROW. And one day, Little
Gorilla was BIG!

And everybody came, and everybody sang
"Happy Birthday Little Gorilla!"

And everybody still loved him.

Everything Grows

by Raffi

Everything grows and grows.

Babies do, animals too.

Everything grows.

Everything grows and grows.

Sisters do, brothers too.

Everything grows.

 Try It Out

Make a class list of things that grow.

Tell what you learned.

1. Look at the pictures. What happens
when you grow and change?

2 years old   6 years old

2. Draw a picture. Show an animal
you've seen grow. Tell how it
changed.

3. Draw a picture to show how Little
Gorilla looked at his birthday party.
Tell what happened to Little Gorilla.

At School

Tell what you know.

How do children get to school?

The Wheels on the Bus

The wheels on the bus go round and round
Round and round, round and round.
The wheels on the bus go round and round
All around the town.

Talk About It

How do you get to school?

Who do we see at school?

Word Bank

classroom

library

office

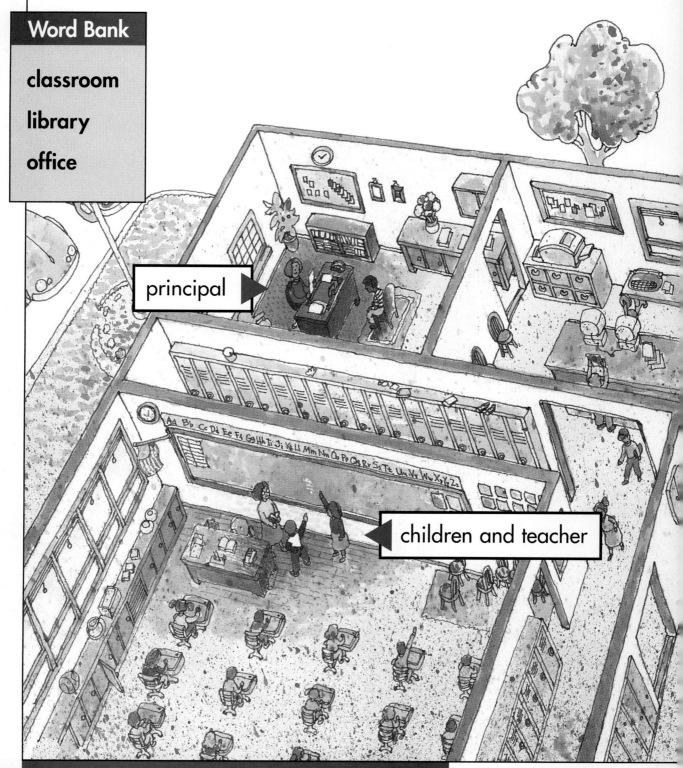

principal ▶

◀ children and teacher

Where are the children
and the teacher?

Where is the principal?

Where is the librarian?

Where is the nurse?

nurse

librarian

Talk About It

Who do you see
at your school?

What do we do at school?

We listen.

We talk.

We read.

We think.

We draw.

We write.

We share.

We play.

We take turns.

We Chant.

When do we go to school?
Monday, Tuesday, Wednesday,
Thursday, and Friday too.
I think it's fun, don't you?

Draw About It

Draw something
you do at school.

What are rules?

Rules tell us what to do.

Your school has rules.

Come to school on time.

Listen to your teacher.

Games have rules.

Take turns. ▶

Jump over the rope. ▶

? Think About It

Why do we have rules?

How many?

Word Bank

1 one
2 two
3 three
4 four
5 five
6 six
7 seven
8 eight
9 nine
10 ten

How many children are listening?

How many children
are reading? ▶

How many children are writing?
▼

My School, Your School

by Bette Birnbaum

Here I am at my school. That's me at my
desk, saying good morning to my teacher.
My teacher's name is Mrs. Siegal.

What is your teacher's name?

Here I am at my school. That's me saying "O." My teacher is playing an alphabet game with us.

What games do you play in school?

Here I am at my school. That's me and Billy with a shape puzzle. We like working together. We are best friends.

Who are your friends at school?

Here I am at my school. That's me writing a story at the computer. I like to write stories about dinosaurs.

What do you like to write about?

Here I am at my school. That's me in the middle circle. After lunch I like to play in the school yard with my friends.

What do you like to do after lunch?

Here I am at my school. That's me coloring in my math workbook. Math is what I like to do best at school.

What do you like to do best at school?

Here I am at my school. That's me playing the maracas. For music we usually sing songs, but today we are playing instruments.

What does your class do for music?

Here I am at my school. That's me in the wolf costume. Can you guess what play we are putting on? Putting on plays is one of the special things we do at school.

What special things do you do at school?

Here I am at my school. That's me reading a book to my friends. Sometimes we read at the end of the day.

When do you read books in school?

Here I am after school. That's me with my friend Tasha at the bus stop across the street from my house. My mom is waiting for us. I can't wait to tell her all about my day!

What will you tell about your day?

The First Day of School

by Sarah Wilson

Hello, hello.
I'm new. Are you?
I'm shy, but I'm
excited, too.

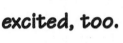

I'm going to sing
and string a kite
and run and jump
and read and write

and talk about
the stars in space
and make new friends!
I like this place!

Try It Out

Act out the poem
as you say it.

Tell what you learned.

1. Name one rule you follow at your school.

2. Who do you see in the pictures? What are they doing?

3. Draw a picture. Show what you like best at school.

Learning

Tell what you know.

What do you **learn** in school?

The Alphabet Song

A, B, C, D, E, F, G,
H, I, J, K, L, M, N, O, P,
Q, R, S, T, U, V,
W, X, Y, and Z.
Now you've heard my ABCs.
Tell me what you think of me.

Talk About It

What letters are in your name?

Name some other letters you know.

What do we learn in school?

We learn to think.

We learn to ▶
read.

◀ We learn to
write.

We learn to ▶
count.

◀ We learn to read maps and globes.

We learn about ▶ people.

◀ We learn about other living things.

We learn from each other.

 Talk About It

What do you do at school?

We practice in school.

Practice means to do something many times.

We learn how to do things by practicing them.

◀ We practice singing songs.

We practice playing ▶ games.

◀ We practice writing words.

We practice speaking ▶
words.

◀ We practice acting out stories.

Draw About It

Draw something you practice at school.

What can you do alone?

Word Bank

run

skip

walk

I can write.

I can read.

I can draw.

What can you do in a group?

I can listen to someone read.

I can draw a picture.

I can play a game.

Talk About It

What do you do alone?

What do you do in groups?

How do children feel at school?

Children have different **feelings** at different times.

Maya is happy today. She likes school.

Samuel is sad today.
He misses his friend.

Paul is scared today.
He is a new student.

❓ Think About It

How can you help
a new student
who is scared?

I Like School

Mayeline Bonilla
age 7

I like school because it's fun. We do fun things like art and gym. We also go to the park.

In my class, we put together a city.
I made a house.

I like to do fun things in my
classroom. I like to do fun things
with my teacher.

If You're Happy

and You Know It

If you're happy and you know it,
clap your hands (**clap, clap**).

If you're happy and you know it,
clap your hands (**clap, clap**).

If you're happy and you know it,
then your face will surely show it.

If you're happy and you know it,
clap your hands (**clap, clap**).

Try It Out

Think of other verses to the song.

Sing them together.

Tell what you learned.

1. Name something you learn in school. How are you learning it?

2. What are the children doing? Are they alone or in a group?

3. Draw a picture. Show something fun to do in a group. Tell about your picture.

Neighbors

Tell what you know.

Where do people live?

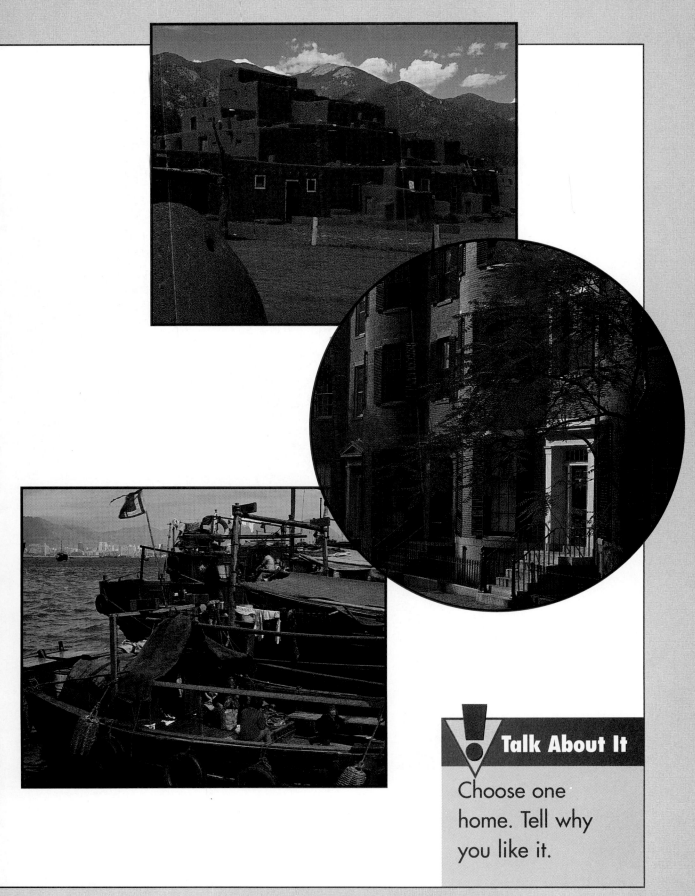

Talk About It

Choose one
home. Tell why
you like it.

What is a neighborhood?

A **neighborhood** is a place where families live near each other.

What are neighbors?

Neighbors are people who live near each other.

Neighbors help each other.

Neighbors can play together too.

Talk About It

How do people work and play together in your neighborhood?

How do maps help us?

Maps show us where to find places.

A neighborhood map shows streets and houses.

Word Bank

house

school

street

Talk About It

Tell what you see in this neighborhood.

What is a community?

A **community** is bigger than a neighborhood.

A community is where groups of people live and work.

A community has houses, apartments, and other places.

PINE

OAK

2nd Street

1st Street

FIRE DEPT.

fire station

Pizza Joint

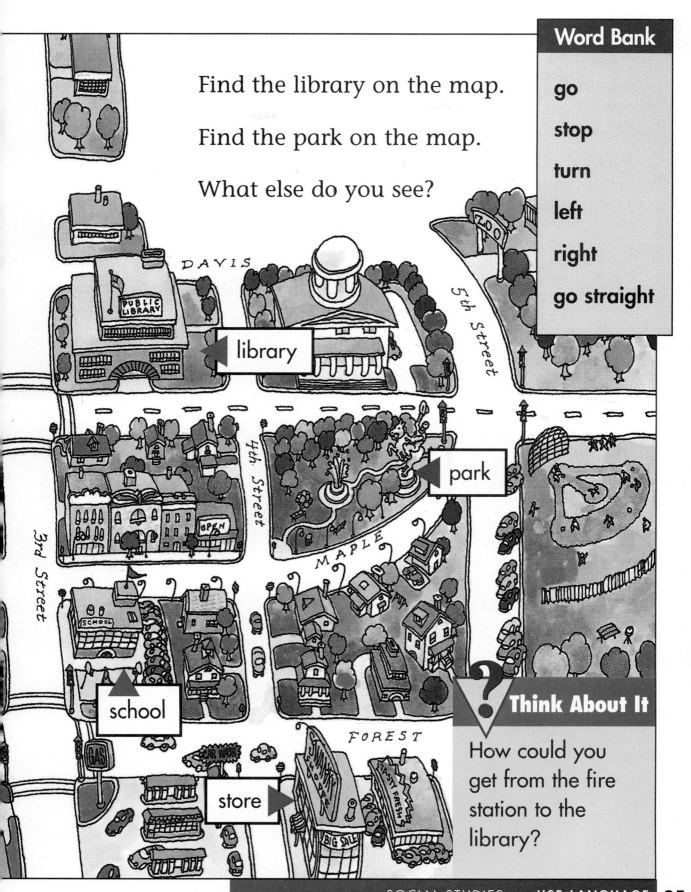

Find the library on the map.

Find the park on the map.

What else do you see?

Word Bank

go

stop

turn

left

right

go straight

library

park

school

store

? Think About It

How could you get from the fire station to the library?

What animals live in a park?

Squirrels can live in a park.

Ducks can live in a park.

pigeons ▶

ducks ▶

How many ducks are in this picture?

How many squirrels are in this picture?

robin ▶

chipmunks ▼

squirrels ▲

Draw About It

Draw a picture of animals that live in a park near you.

One Afternoon

by Yumi Heo

Minho liked to do errands with his mother.

One afternoon, they went to the Laundromat
to drop off their clothes and then to the
beauty salon to get his mother's hair cut.

At the ice cream store, Minho got a vanilla cone.

They looked in the pet store window at
the puppies, kittens, hamsters, and birds.

They picked up his father's shoes at the shoe repair store and got food for dinner at the supermarket.

Last of all, Minho and his mother went
back to the Laundromat to get the clothes
they had dropped off.

Traffic was very heavy on the street because of the construction.

CONNECT LANGUAGE • SOCIAL STUDIES/LITERATURE

A fire engine tried to get through.

The El train was passing by above.

Near Minho's apartment, children were
playing stickball.

Minho and his mother were very happy to be back in their quiet home. Minho was tired and fell asleep on the couch.

But from the bathroom . . .

PLUNK!

My Street

words and music by Malvina Reynolds

My street is a friendly street,
People say hello to the people they meet,
People walk along with the happy feet
On my street, Yes.
Little kids, big kids, the women and men,
Know you by your name and they knew you when,
Know where you're going and where you've been,
On my street, Yes!

"My Street" words and music by Malvina Reynolds from THERE'S MUSIC IN THE AIR by Malvina Reynolds.
Copyright © 1972 Schroder Music Co. (ASCAP) All rights reserved. Reprinted by permission of Schroder Music Co.

HOLA   CIAO   SHALOM   CHÀO EM

Try It Out

Say **hello** in two languages.

Tell what you learned.

1. What do neighbors do together?

2. Look at the map. What is near
the school?

3. Name a place Minho and his
mother went.

Animals and Their Homes

Tell what you know.

Where can animals live?

Talk About It

What other animals could live in this place?

What animals do you see?

Name the animals.

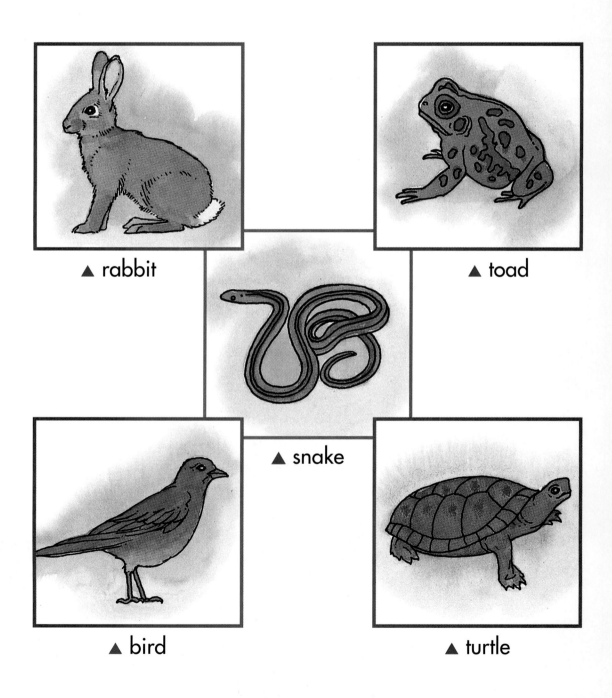

▲ rabbit

▲ toad

▲ snake

▲ bird

▲ turtle

Where do these animals live?

Which animals live in a pond?

Which animals live in a field?

Which animals live in a tree?

birds ▲

rabbits ▼

toads ▶

Draw About It

Draw an animal you have seen. Tell where it lives.

What animals live at a zoo?

The seal swims in water.

The monkey climbs in trees.

◀ seal

monkey ▶

lion ▶

bears ▼

Word Bank

camel

chimpanzee

giraffe

gorilla

tiger

The lion rests in tall grass.

The bears play on rocks.

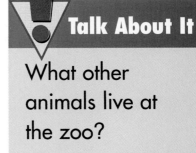

Talk About It

What other animals live at the zoo?

How do animals use trees for homes?

Some animals live on the branches of a tree.

Some animals live in holes in a tree.

Some animals live on the leaves of a tree.

caterpillar ▼

squirrel ▶

raccoon ▶

◄ opossum

◄ woodpecker

Birds build nests in trees.

This bird builds a big nest.

This bird builds a small nest.

This bird builds a nest that looks like a basket.

? Think About It

Why do some birds build big nests?
Why do some birds build small nests?

How many pets?

Some people keep animals as pets.

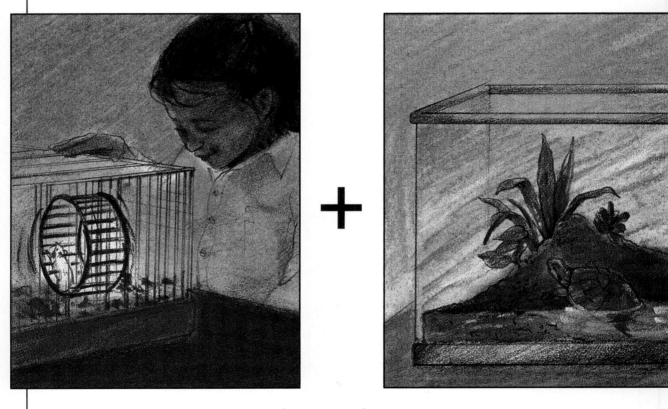

Laura has one mouse and one turtle.
How many pets does she have in all?

Marcus has one dog.
The dog has three puppies.
How many pets does Marcus have in all?

Olivia has four kittens.
She gave one to Bobby.
How many kittens does Olivia have left?

Talk About It

Tell about a pet
you would like to
have. Tell where
your pet might live.

Taking Care of Pets

Pets need their owners to care
for them.
They need food, water, exercise,
and a place to sleep.

How will the boy take care of his puppy?

The boy will give food to his puppy.

The boy will give water to his puppy.

The boy will take his puppy out for exercise.

The boy will make a cozy bed for his puppy.

Talk About It

How would you care for a puppy?

The Furry Home

by J. M. Westrup

If I were a mouse
And wanted a house
I think I would choose
My new red shoes.
Furry edges,
Fur inside,
What a lovely
Place to hide!
I'd not travel,
I'd not roam—
Just sit in
My furry home.

Try It Out

Pretend you are
a mouse.
Draw your house.

Tell what you learned.

1. Name two places animals can live.

2. Make a web like this one. Add the names of animals that live in each place.

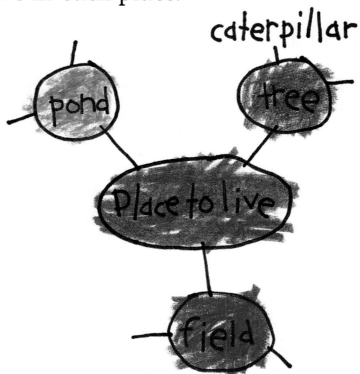

caterpillar

pond

tree

Place to live

field

3. A pet needs water. What else does a pet need?

How You Can Feel Safe

Tell what you know.

Where is **safety** important?

▲ street

▲ car

▲ playground

▲ bus

soccer field ▲

beach ▶

Talk About It

Name other places where safety is important.

Who helps keep you safe?

▲ Teachers keep us safe at school.

▲ Park rangers keep us safe in the park.

▲ Coaches keep us safe on the ball field.

Our families keep us safe at home.

Police officers keep us safe on the streets.

Word Bank

baby-sitter

crossing guard

firefighters

Think About It

Name other people who keep you safe. What do they do?

How can you cross the street safely?

Obey the traffic lights.

Wait for the green light.

Walk in the **crosswalk.**

Cross at the corner.

Look both ways.

Wait for **traffic** to pass.

Draw About It

Draw a traffic light that shows go.

Draw a traffic light that shows stop.

How can you stay safe in a car?

Always use a seat belt.

Always keep your head and arms in the car.

Don't bother the driver.

How can you stay safe on the playground?

Take turns.

Do not push.

Do not talk to strangers.

Keep out of the way of others.

 Talk About It

Tell how you keep safe.

What are germs?

Germs are very small.

You cannot see them.

Some germs make you sick.

You can wash germs away.

When can a doctor help you?

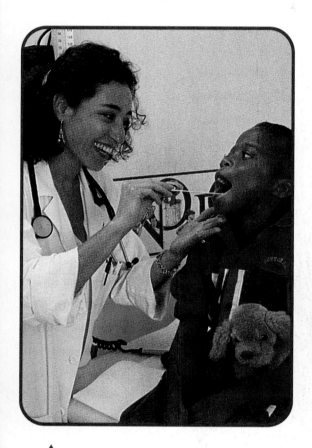

▲

A **doctor** can help you when you are sick.

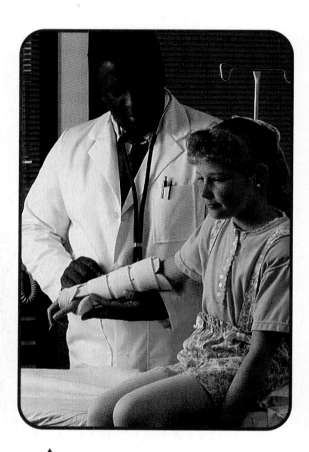

▲

A doctor can help you when you are hurt.

Talk About It

Tell about a time a doctor helped you.

The Lady with the Alligator Purse

Adapted and illustrated by Nadine Bernard Westcott

Miss Lucy had a baby,
His name was Tiny Tim,

She put him in the bathtub
To see if he could swim.

He drank up all the water,
He ate up all the soap,

He tried to eat the bathtub,
But it wouldn't go down his throat.

Miss Lucy called the doctor,

Miss Lucy called the nurse,

Miss Lucy called the lady
With the alligator purse.

In came the doctor,
In came the nurse,
In came the lady
With the alligator purse.

"Mumps," said the doctor,
"Measles," said the nurse,

"Nonsense!" said the lady
With the alligator purse.

"Penicillin," said the doctor,
"Castor oil," said the nurse,

"Pizza!" said the lady
With the alligator purse.

Look Both Ways

by Dee Lillegard

I never run across the street—
I always stop to see
If something big is coming in
The direction of *me*.

You never know—
There might be cars.
There also might be
DINOSAURS!

And what if one
Should step on me!
That's why I always
Stop to see.

Try It Out

Name an action for friends to do.
Say "Green Light" to start.
Say "Red Light" to stop.

Tell what you learned.

1. Name some workers who help keep you safe.

2. Tell what you do before you cross a street.

3. Draw a picture to show the three people Miss Lucy called to help Tiny Tim.

How You Can Feel Healthy

Tell what you know.

What are they doing?

Why are these things good to do?

Word Bank

drink

sleep

wash

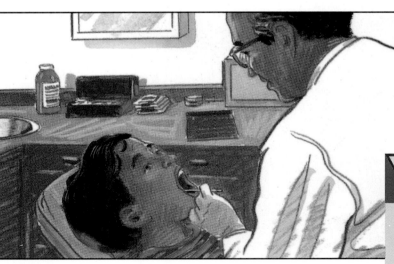

Talk About It

What do you do to feel healthy?

Why is it good to exercise?

How do they get **exercise?**

How does this help them?

Word Bank

bike

hike

skate

skip

swim

There are other ways to exercise too.

Work with a partner.
Make a list.
Share it with the class.

Talk About It

How do you like
to exercise?

Keeping Healthy

Ask a partner.

What are they doing to keep **healthy?**

How does this help?

How do you keep clean and healthy?

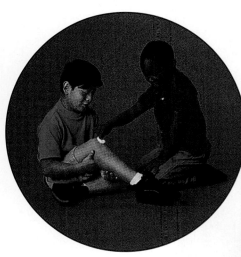

Make a class list.

Tell what you do.

? Think About It

What would you do if you cut your knee?

What kinds of foods help you grow and be healthy?

You need some of these foods each day.

What kinds of foods do you need most?

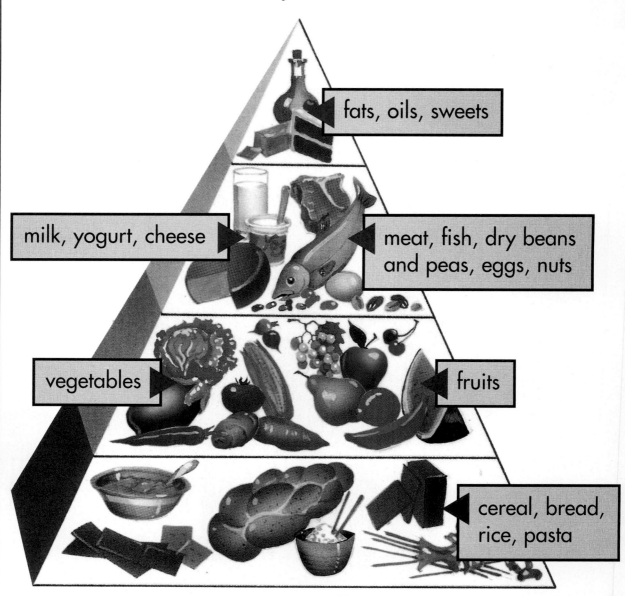

fats, oils, sweets

milk, yogurt, cheese

meat, fish, dry beans and peas, eggs, nuts

vegetables

fruits

cereal, bread, rice, pasta

Make a food chart.

1. Draw **vegetables** on one side.

2. Draw **fruits** on the other side.

Word Bank

beans

grapes

oranges

peas

potatoes

! Talk About It

What vegetables do you like?

What fruits do you like?

How many in all?

Maria's Chart

Monday	
Tuesday	
Wednesday	
Thursday	
Friday	

How many carrots did Maria eat in all?

Shu's Chart

Monday	
Tuesday	
Wednesday	
Thursday	
Friday	

How many bowls of soup did Shu eat in all?

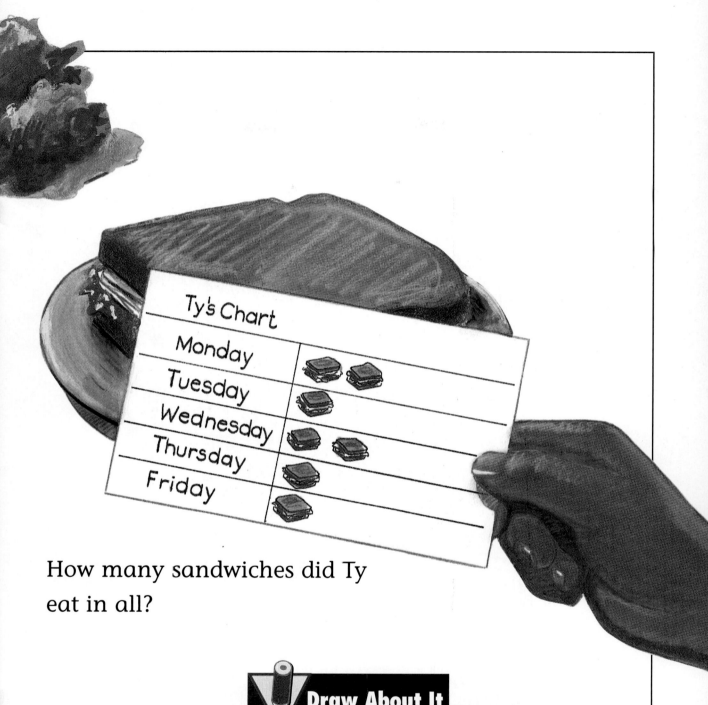

Ty's Chart	
Monday	
Tuesday	
Wednesday	
Thursday	
Friday	

How many sandwiches did Ty eat in all?

Draw About It

Draw the sandwiches Ty ate on Thursday and Friday. Make up a number sentence. How many sandwiches did he eat in all?

Allie Alligator

by Babs Bell Hajdusiewicz

When all the other alligators
went off for a swim,
Little Allie Alligator
went into the gym.

She saw giraffes play basketball.
  She saw the foxes run.
She saw gorillas climb the ropes
  and then when they were done . . .

Allie tried to climb the ropes.
  She tried to throw the ball.
She tried to run around the track,
  but alligators crawl!

So Allie ran to get her suit
　　and crawled into the pool.
"I'm glad I'm long and flat," she said.
"And swimming makes me cool."

Try It Out

Act out an exercise you like to do. Ask classmates to guess what exercise you are doing.

Tell what you learned.

1. What do you do to stay healthy?

2. Name some foods that help you grow and stay healthy.

3. What was Allie good at? How did Allie feel at the end of the story?

Using Our Senses

Tell what you know.

What can you see?

What can you hear?

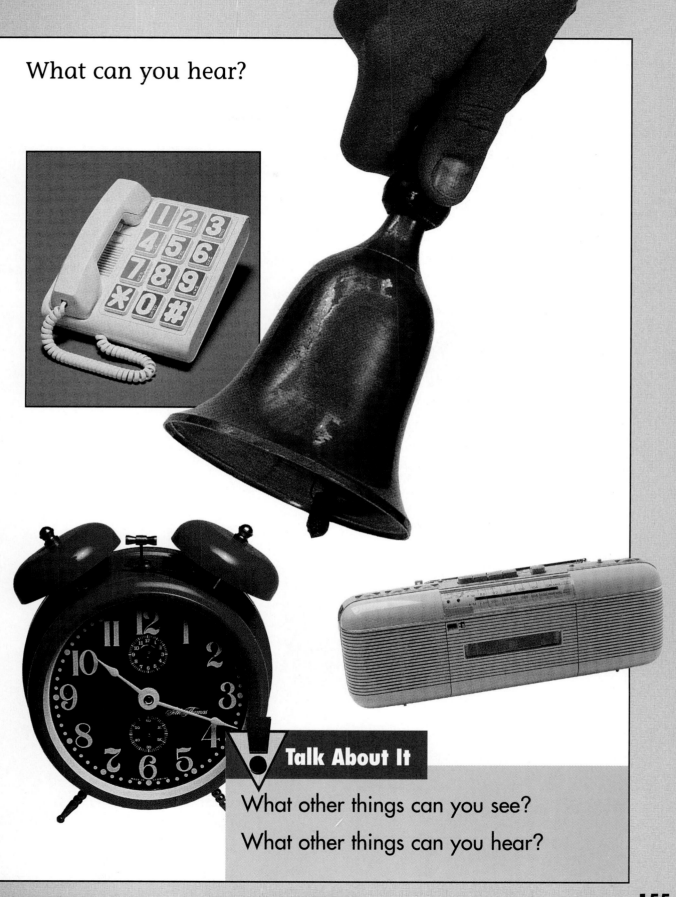

What other things can you see?

What other things can you hear?

155

Senses and Body Parts

What's happening in the park?

She sees a butterfly.

She hears a bird.

She smells flowers.

He feels the water.

Make a class chart.
Tell which part of the
body is used.

Sense	Body Part
hear	
see	
taste	
smell	
touch	

He tastes an apple.

eye

nose

tongue

hand

ear

Word Bank

ball

bat

children

rope

Talk About It

You are in the
park. What else
can you see, hear,
touch, or taste?

What can your senses tell you?

ball   bird

You see colors and shapes.

What is round?
What is red?

kitten   lion

You hear sounds.

What is loud?
What is soft?

skunk

flower

You smell things.

What smells good?
What smells bad?

lemon

pretzel

You taste things.

What tastes sour?
What tastes salty?

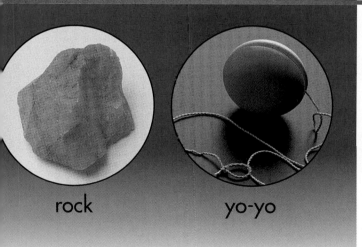

rock

yo-yo

You touch things.

What feels smooth?
What feels bumpy?

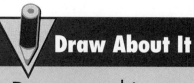

Draw About It

Draw something
you like to taste.

How can you take care of your eyes and ears?

Wear sunglasses on sunny days.

Never look right at the sun.

Cover your ears when you're near loud sounds.

Turn down loud music.

How do these workers take
care of their eyes and ears?

? **Think About It**

Why should you
take care of your
eyes and ears?

Make high and low sounds.

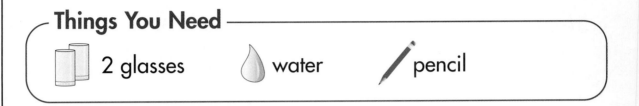

Things You Need

2 glasses   water   pencil

Follow these steps.

1. Fill the first glass almost to the top.

2. Fill the second glass halfway.

3. Tap each glass with the pencil.

4. Which sounds higher?

My Record

The first glass sounds _____.

The second glass sounds _____.

Think About It

How would you make the sound lower?

Peace at Last

by Jill Murphy

The hour was late.
Mr. Bear was tired,
Mrs. Bear was tired,
and Baby Bear was tired,
so they all went to bed.
Mrs. Bear fell asleep.
Mr. Bear didn't.
Mrs. Bear began to snore.

"SNORE," went Mrs. Bear.
"SNORE, SNORE, SNORE."
"Oh, NO!" said Mr. Bear,
"I can't stand THIS."
So he got up and went to
sleep in Baby Bear's room.

Baby Bear was not asleep either.
He was lying in bed, pretending
to be an airplane.
"NYAAOW!" went Baby Bear.
"NYAAOW! NYAAOW!"
"Oh, NO!" said Mr. Bear,
"I can't stand THIS."
So he got up
and went to sleep in the living room.

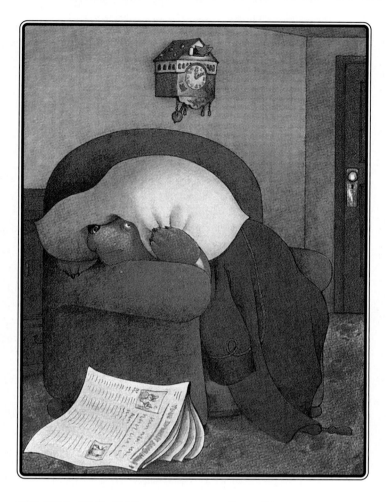

TICK-TOCK...went the living room
clock....TICK-TOCK, TICK-TOCK,
CUCKOO! CUCKOO!
"Oh, NO!" said Mr. Bear,
"I can't stand THIS."
So he went off to sleep in the kitchen.

DRIP, DRIP…went the leaky kitchen
faucet.
HMMMMMMMMMM…
went the refrigerator.
"Oh, NO!" said Mr. Bear,
"I can't stand THIS."
So he got up
and went to sleep in the garden.

Well, you would not believe
what noises there are in
the garden at night.
"TOO-WHIT-TOO-WHOO!"
went the owl.
"SNUFFLE, SNUFFLE," went
the hedgehog.
"MIAAAOW!" sang the cats
on the wall.
"Oh, NO!" said Mr. Bear,
"I can't stand THIS."
So he went off to sleep in
the car.

It was cold in the car
and uncomfortable, but
Mr. Bear was so tired
that he didn't notice.
He was just falling asleep
when all the birds started to
sing and the sun peeped in at
the window.
"TWEET TWEET!" went the birds.
SHINE, SHINE…went the sun.
"Oh, NO!" said Mr. Bear,
"I can't stand THIS."
So he got up and went back
into the house.

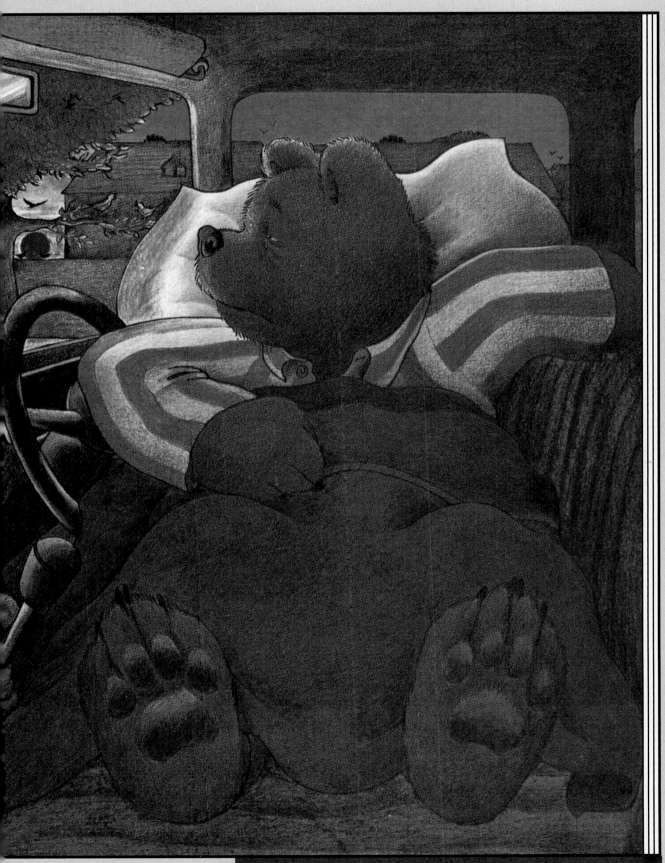

In the house Baby Bear was
fast asleep, and Mrs. Bear had
turned over and wasn't snoring
anymore.
Mr. Bear got into bed and closed
his eyes.
"Peace at last," he said to himself.
BRRRRRRRRRRRRRRR...went the
alarm clock. BRRRRRR!

Mrs. Bear sat up and rubbed her eyes.

"Good morning, dear," she said.

"Did you sleep well?"

"Not VERY well, dear," yawned Mr. Bear.

"Never mind," said Mrs. Bear.

"I'll bring you the mail and a nice
cup of tea."

And she did.

The Bear Went Over the Mountain

Oh, the bear went over the mountain,
The bear went over the mountain,
The bear went over the mountain
To see what he could see.

To see what he could see,
To see what he could see,

Oh, the bear went over the mountain,
The bear went over the mountain,
The bear went over the mountain
To see what he could see.

▼✋ Try It Out

Think of something the bear might see.
Give clues to help classmates guess
what you are thinking of.

Tell what you learned.

1. Make a chart. Tell what each body part helps you do.

Part of My Body	Helps Me
eyes	see
ears	
nose	
tongue	
hands	

2. How can you take care of your eyes?

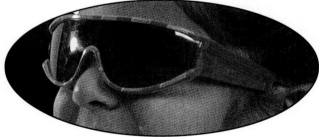

3. Why couldn't Mr. Bear sleep?

CHAPTER 10

How We See and Hear

Tell what you know.

Look at the red line and the blue line.
Which is longer?
Which is shorter?

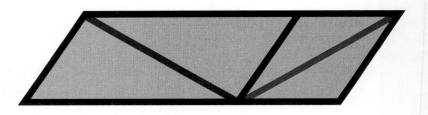

Look at the two lines.
Which is longer?
Which is shorter?

Use your ruler. Check your guess.

Which makes a louder sound?

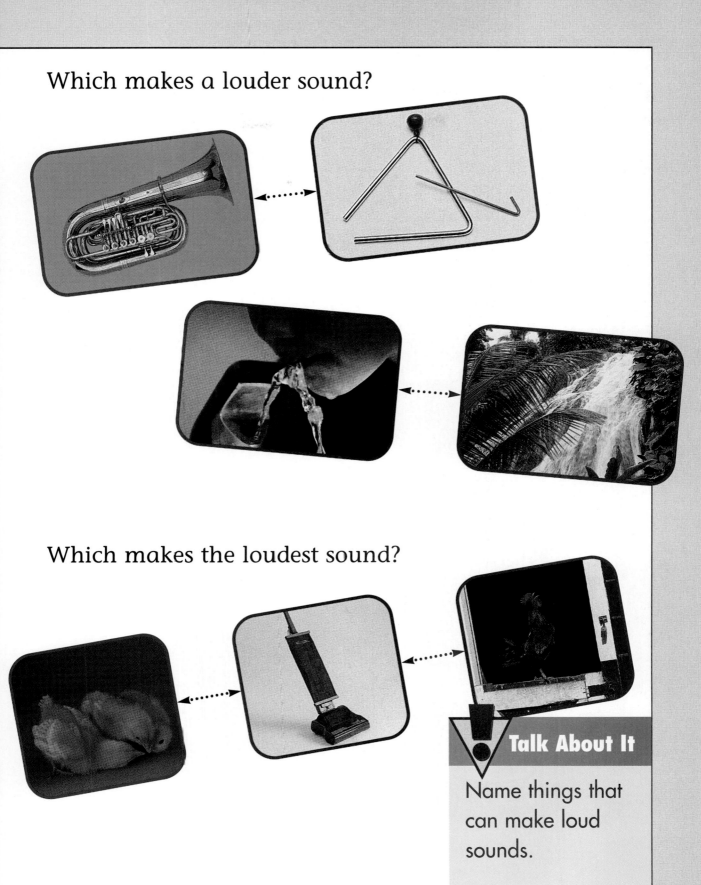

Which makes the loudest sound?

Talk About It

Name things that can make loud sounds.

179

How do people and animals see?

People use their eyes to see.
Animals use their eyes too.

Some animals see very well at night.
When do people see best?

People have two eyes.

Most animals have two eyes.
But spiders have eight eyes.

▲ cat

▲ eagle

▲ rabbit

▲ spider

Word Bank

glasses

lights

magnifying
glass

sunglasses

Think About It

What things do
people use to help
them see better?

How do people and animals hear?

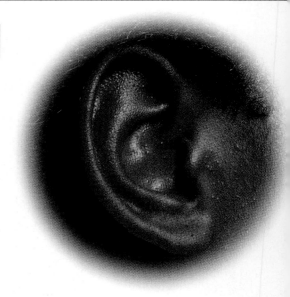

People use their ears to hear.
Most animals use their ears to hear too.
Some animals hear very well.

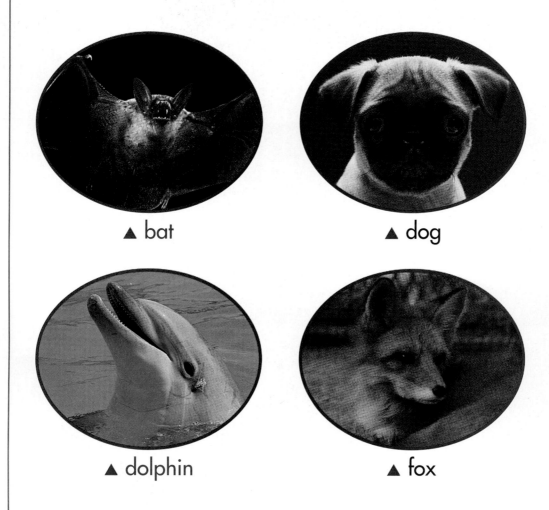

▲ bat

▲ dog

▲ dolphin

▲ fox

Some animals have very big ears.

Some animals' ears cannot be seen.

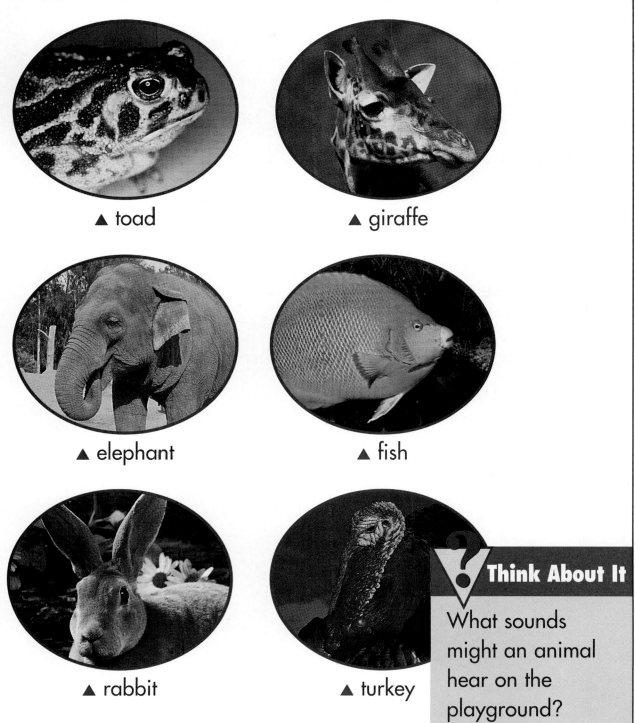

▲ toad

▲ giraffe

▲ elephant

▲ fish

▲ rabbit

▲ turkey

Think About It

What sounds might an animal hear on the playground?

Do you see better with two eyes?

Let's find out.

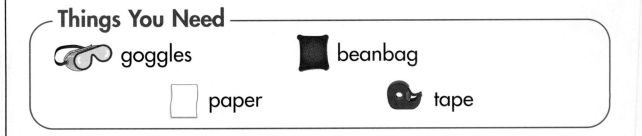

Things You Need

goggles

beanbag

paper

tape

Follow these steps.

1. Have a partner toss a beanbag to you 10 times.

2. Count the times you catch it.

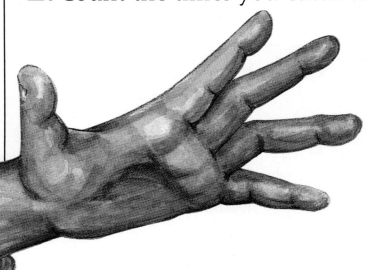

3. Tape paper over one side of the goggles.

4. Put the goggles on.

5. Have a partner toss the beanbag to you 10 times.

6. Count the times you catch it.

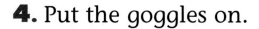

	number of times beanbag was caught
using 1 eye	
using 2 eyes	

Write About It

Make a chart like this one. Write how many times you caught the beanbag.

How many things do you see?

Look at the picture.

How many police cars do you see?

How many green cars do you see?

How many fire engines do you see?

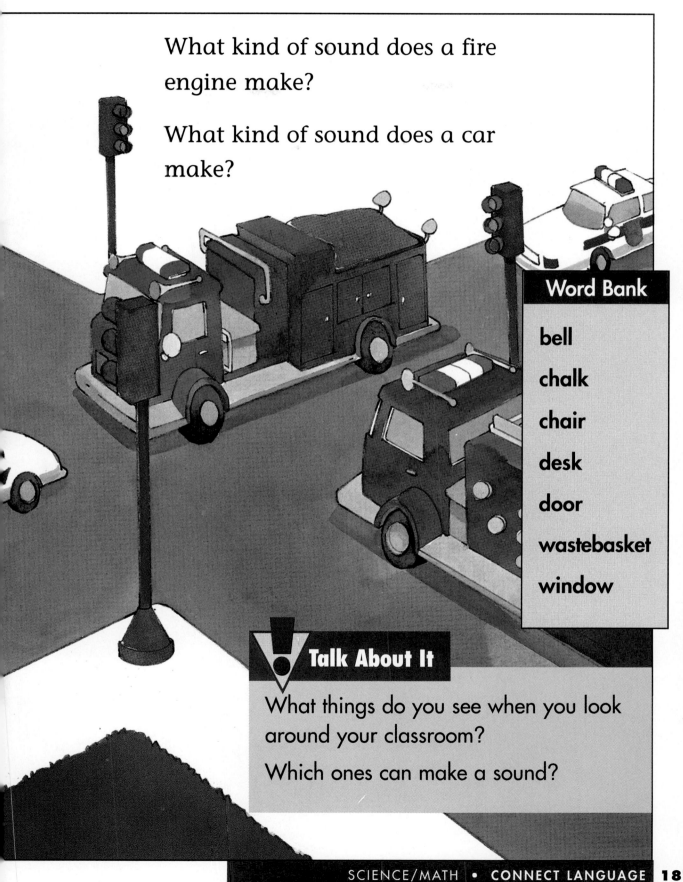

What kind of sound does a fire engine make?

What kind of sound does a car make?

Word Bank

bell

chalk

chair

desk

door

wastebasket

window

Talk About It

What things do you see when you look around your classroom?

Which ones can make a sound?

Hi,

I am having fun here. I saw a parade with a giant dragon. The bands were very noisy. TOOT! TOOT! BOOM! BOOM!

Love,
Michael

My Friend
300 Main Street
Happytown, U.S.A.
12345

Write About It

Write a postcard. Tell about a place you have been.

What did you see and hear?

The Clap and Quiet Poem

The Clap and Quiet Poem

by Dee Lillegard

Clap, clap, clap . . .

My hands make noise.

Clap, clap, clap . . .

Let's hear the boys.

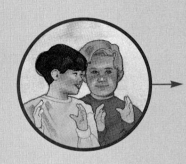

Clap, clap, clap . . .

Now girls clap too.

Clap, clap, clap . . .

And now we're through!

Quiet hands.

Quiet face.

Let's have quiet

Every place.

Try It Out

Shhh . . .

Write some more
lines for this poem.

Tell what you learned.

1. Name one thing that makes a loud sound. Name one thing that makes a soft sound.

2. Can you see better with one eye or with two eyes?

3. Draw a picture of a place you have been. Show things you saw and heard. Label your picture.

CHAPTER 11

The Four Seasons

Tell what you know.

What are the months of the year?

January							February							March						
S	M	T	W	T	F	S	S	M	T	W	T	F	S	S	M	T	W	T	F	S
1	2	3	4	5	6	7						1	2						3	4
8	9	10	11	12	13	14	5	6	7	8	9	10	11	5	6	7	8	9	10	11
15	16	17	18	19	20	21	12	13	14	15	16	17	18	12	13	14	15	16	17	18
22	23	24	25	26	27	28	19	20	21	22	23	24	25	19	20	21	22	23	24	25
29	30	31					26	27	28					26	27	28	29	30	31	

April							May							June						
S	M	T	W	T	F	S	S	M	T	W	T	F	S	S	M	T	W	T	F	S
						1		1	2	3	4	5	6						1	2
2	3	4	5	6	7	8	7	8	9	10	11	12	13	4	5	6	7	8	9	10
9	10	11	12	13	14	15	14	15	16	17	18	19	20	11	12	13	14	15	16	17
16	17	18	19	20	21	22	21	22	23	24	25	26	27	18	19	20	21	22	23	24
23/30	24	25	26	27	28	29	28	29	30	31				25	26	27	28	29	30	

July							August							September						
S	M	T	W	T	F	S	S	M	T	W	T	F	S	S	M	T	W	T	F	S
						1			1	2	3	4	5						1	2
2	3	4	5	6	7	8	6	7	8	9	10	11	12	3	4	5	6	7	8	9
9	10	11	12	13	14	15	13	14	15	16	17	18	19	10	11	12	13	14	15	16
16	17	18	19	20	21	22	20	21	22	23	24	25	26	17	18	19	20	21	22	23
23/30	24/31	25	26	27	28	29	27	28	29	30	31			24	25	26	27	28	29	30

October							November							December						
S	M	T	W	T	F	S	S	M	T	W	T	F	S	S	M	T	W	T	F	S
1	2	3	4	5	6	7				1	2	3	4						1	2
8	9	10	11	12	13	14	5	6	7	8	9	10	11	3	4	5	6	7	8	9
15	16	17	18	19	20	21	12	13	14	15	16	17	18	10	11	12	13	14	15	16
22	23	24	25	26	27	28	19	20	21	22	23	24	25	17	18	19	20	21	22	23
29	30	31					26	27	28	29	30			24/31	25	26	27	28	29	30

What are the four seasons of the year?

winter

spring

fall

summer

Talk About It

Which season do you like best? Why?

What is it like in each season?

▲ In most places in the U. S., it is colder in **winter.**

▲ It is warmer in **spring.**

▲ It is hotter in **summer.**

▲ It is cooler in **fall.**

Talk About It

What season is it now?

What is the weather like where you live?

What can you do in different weather?

windy

cloudy

sunny

snowy

rainy

How can you dress for the weather?

◄ What would you wear on a snowy day?

What would you wear ▶
on a rainy day?

◄ What would you wear on a sunny day?

Word Bank

cap

mittens

raincoat

shorts

sweater

T-shirt

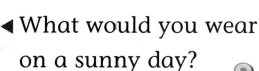

Draw About It

What do you like to do when it is sunny? What do you wear?

Draw a picture.

How does a coat keep you warm?

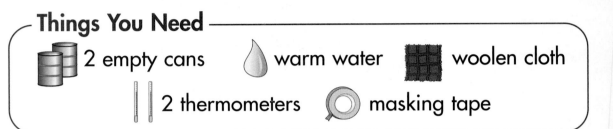

Things You Need

- 2 empty cans
- warm water
- woolen cloth
- 2 thermometers
- masking tape

Follow these steps.

1. Wrap the cloth around one can. Tape the cloth in place.

2. Fill each can with warm water.

3. Put a thermometer in each can.

4. Measure the temperature of the water in each can. Do this every 5 minutes for 20 minutes.

Keep a record.

Make a chart like this.

Write the temperature of the water in each can.

	temperature of water with cloth	temperature of water without cloth
at start		
after 5 minutes		
after 10 minutes		
after 15 minutes		
after 20 minutes		

 **Think About It**

Which can of water stayed warmer?

How is a cloth around a can like a coat you wear on a cold day?

Trees and Seasons

How does this apple tree change
with each season?

▲ There are no leaves
in winter.

▲ There are buds and
blossoms in spring.

▲ Leaves and apples
grow in summer.

▲ Apples are picked.
Leaves change colors
in fall.

Trees in Forests

People like to visit forests in different seasons.

How do people enjoy the forest?

Word Bank

gather

hike

look

ski

Talk About It

How would you like to spend time in the forest?

The Good Morning Weather Report

Good Morning, Chicago!

Here is the weather for this winter day. It is snowy. It is very cold. The temperature is 8 degrees. The wind is blowing hard.

Don't forget to put on your snow boots!

Good Morning, San Francisco!

Here is the weather for this winter day. It is rainy. The temperature is 55 degrees. The wind is blowing softly.

Don't forget to take along a raincoat and umbrella.

Good Morning, Miami!

Here is the weather for this winter day. It is sunny. The temperature is 73 degrees. The wind is blowing softly.

Don't forget to take along your sunglasses and a sun hat.

Good Morning, Dallas!

Here is the weather for this winter day. It is cloudy and cool. The temperature is 35 degrees. The wind is blowing hard.

Don't forget to wear a warm jacket.

Talk About It

Which place is most like where you live?

You'll Sing A Song

Words and music by Ella Jenkins

You'll sing a song,
And I'll sing a song,
And we'll sing a song together.

You'll sing a song,
And I'll sing a song,
In warm or wintry weather.

You'll play a tune,
And I'll play a tune,
And we'll play a tune together.

You'll play a tune,
And I'll play a tune,
In warm or wintry weather.

Try It Out

Make up new
verses for the song
to sing together.

Tell what you learned.

1. What are the four seasons?

2. What are the people doing? What season is it?

3. Draw a picture of winter where you live. Show what you are wearing.

CHAPTER 12

Trees

Tell what you know.

Who needs trees?

Talk About It

What animals live
near trees where
you live?

How do people use trees?

▲ People cut down trees for wood.

▲ People burn wood to make heat.

▲ People build things from wood.

Word Bank

blocks

chairs

door

floor

houses

paper

pencils

toys

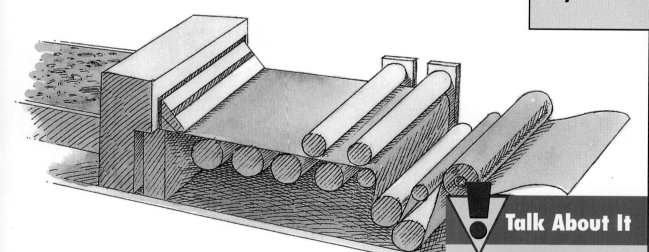

▲ People make paper from wood.

People use wood in many ways.

Talk About It

Look around. Name other things that are made of wood.

How can we save trees?

People cut down trees to make paper.

People can **recycle** paper to save trees.

To recycle means to use again.

How do the children recycle the paper?

People can protect trees from fire.

People can plant new trees.

Talk About It

How can you save paper?

How are trees alike and different?

Different kinds of trees grow in different places.

Palm trees grow in ▶ warm places.

◀ Willow trees grow in warm and cold places.

Pine trees grow in warm ▶ and cold places.

How are leaves alike and different?

The leaves of different trees have different shapes.

Collect different kinds of leaves.

Group the leaves that are alike.

How many groups do you have?

Draw About It

Draw one group of leaves you found.

What do tree seeds do?

Tree seeds are different sizes and shapes.

All tree seeds are alike in one way.

All tree seeds can grow into new trees.

Plant a tree seed.

tree seeds   soil   cup

plastic bag   water

Follow these steps.

1. Fill a cup with soil. Water the soil.

2. Plant a tree seed in the soil.

3. Cover the cup with a plastic bag.

4. Put the cup in a warm, sunny place.

5. Add a few drops of water to the soil each day.

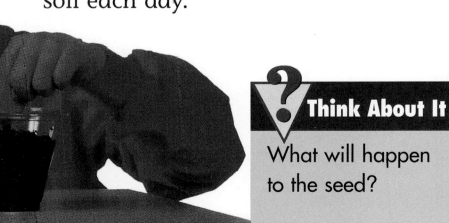

? Think About It

What will happen to the seed?

Trees

by Harry Behn

illustrated by
James Endicott

Trees are the kindest things I know,
They do no harm, they simply grow

And spread a shade for sleepy cows,

And gather birds among their boughs.

They give us fruit in leaves above,

And wood to make our houses of,

And leaves to burn on Hallowe'en,

And in the Spring new buds of green.

They are the first when day's begun
To touch the beams of morning sun.

They are the last to hold the light
When evening changes into night,

And when a moon floats on the sky
They hum a drowsy lullaby

Of sleepy children long ago . . .

Trees are the kindest things I know.

Draw About It

Draw a picture of a tree. Tell a partner about your tree.

Shadows

by Leland B. Jacobs

The shadows of bushes
    Are much too small;
They hardly cover
    A child at all.

But the shadows of trees
    Are long and wide,
So that's the place
    Where I like to hide.

If I hide in the bushes,
    Everyone sees
My arms and hands
    Or my legs and knees.

But deep in the shadow
    Of a tree,
Not even the sun
    Can discover me.

Try It Out

On a sunny day, look at your shadow
in the morning. Look again at noon.
How has it changed?

Tell what you learned.

1. Name two things made from trees.

2. How can you help save trees?

3. Write what you learned about trees when you read the poem "Trees."

Children's
Reference
Section

① Alphabet

Aa

Bb

Cc

Dd

Ee

Ff

Gg

Hh

Ii

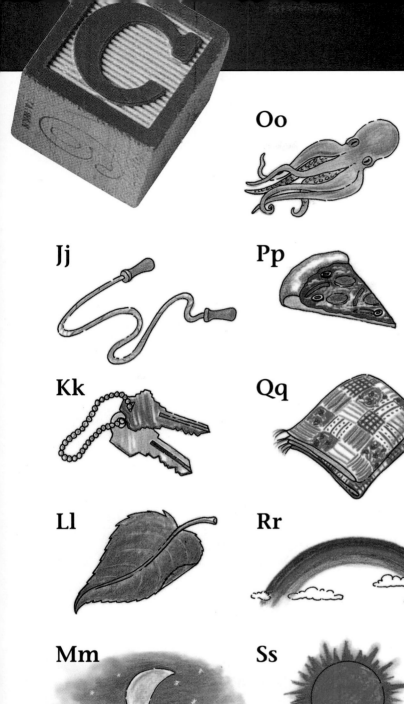

Oo

Uu

Jj

Pp

Vv

Kk

Qq

Ww

Ll

Rr

Xx

Mm

Ss

Yy

Nn

Tt

Zz

② Colors and Shapes

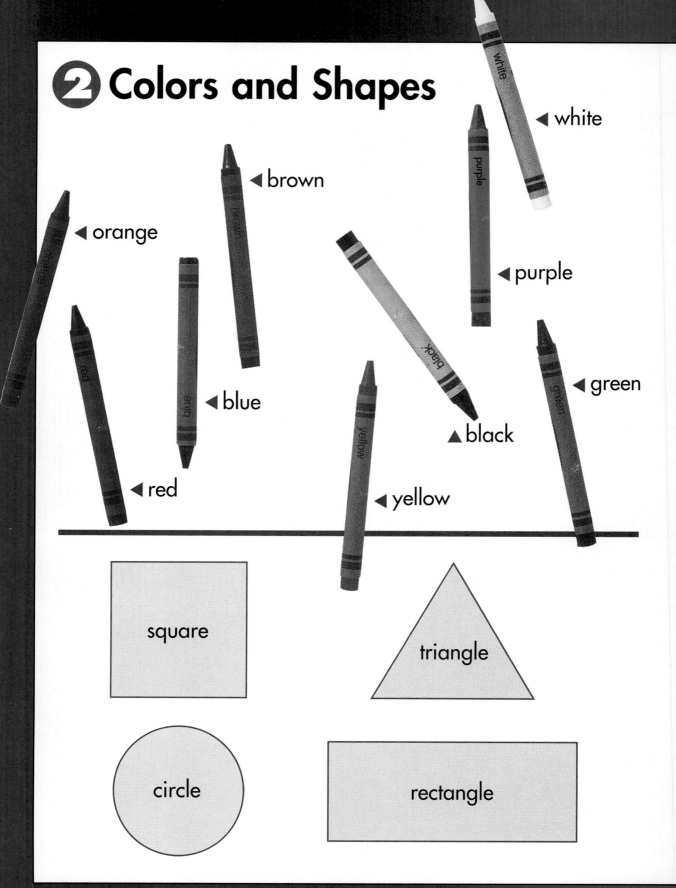

white

brown

orange

purple

blue

green

red

black

yellow

square

triangle

circle

rectangle

3 Numbers

1 one

6 six

2 two

7 seven

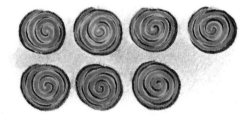

3 three

8 eight

4 four

9 nine

5 five

10 ten

④ Days and Seasons

| | | | November | | | |
SUNDAY	MONDAY	TUESDAY	WEDNESDAY	THURSDAY	FRIDAY	SATURDAY
	1	2	3	4	5	6
7	8	9	10	11	12	13
14	15	16	17	18	19	20
21	22	23	24	25	26	27
28	29	30				

days of week

seasons

winter

fall

summer

spring

⑤ Body Parts

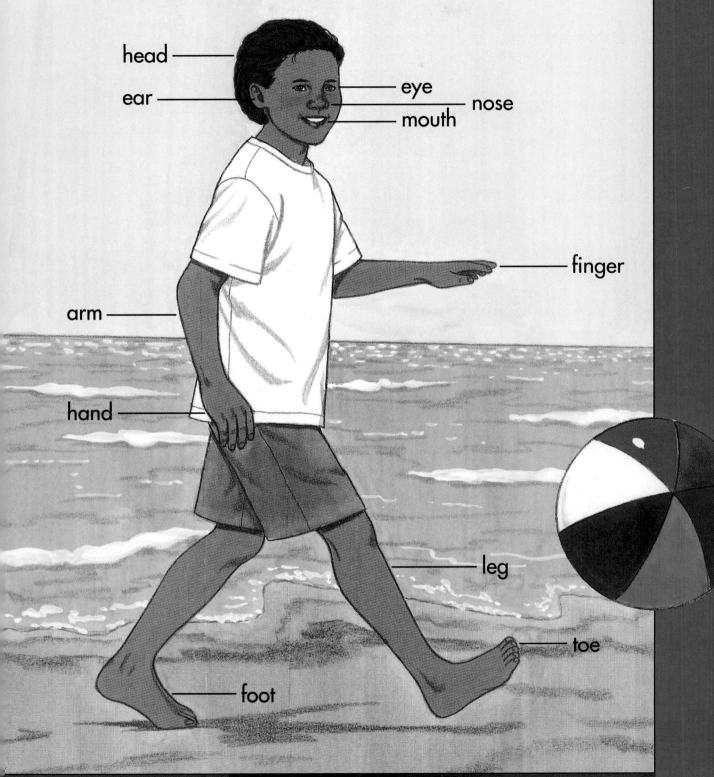

head
ear
eye
nose
mouth
finger
arm
hand
leg
toe
foot

6 Senses

▲ hear

▲ see

▲ touch

◄ smell

▲ taste